This coloring book belongs to

_____

© PAULEY PRESS
All rights reserved

No part of this book may be reproduced, distributed, or transmitted, in any form or by any means, including photocopying, recording, or other electronic or mechanical methods, without prior written permission of the publisher, except in the case of brief quotations embodied in critical reviews and certain other noncommercial uses permitted by copyright law.

Use your fucking blinker, dumbass

PAULEY PRESS

PAULEY PRESS

PAULEY PRESS

PAULEY PRESS

I SWEAR, YOU DRIVE LIKE A FUCKING IDIOT

PAULEY PRESS

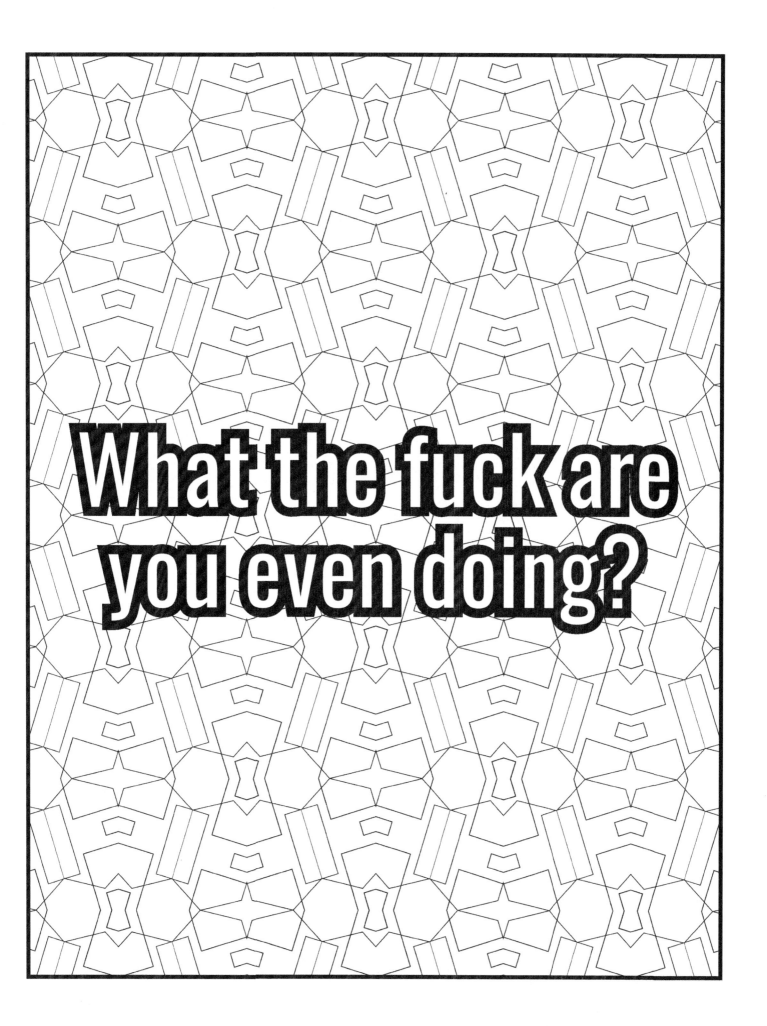

PAULEY PRESS

PAULEY PRESS

PAULEY PRESS

PAULEY PRESS

PAULEY PRESS

PAULEY PRESS

PAULEY PRESS

PAULEY PRESS

PAULEY PRESS

PAULEY PRESS

PAULEY PRESS

PAULEY PRESS

PAULEY PRESS

PAULEY PRESS

PAULEY PRESS

PAULEY PRESS

PAULEY PRESS

PAULEY PRESS

PAULEY PRESS

PAULEY PRESS

PAULEY PRESS

PAULEY PRESS

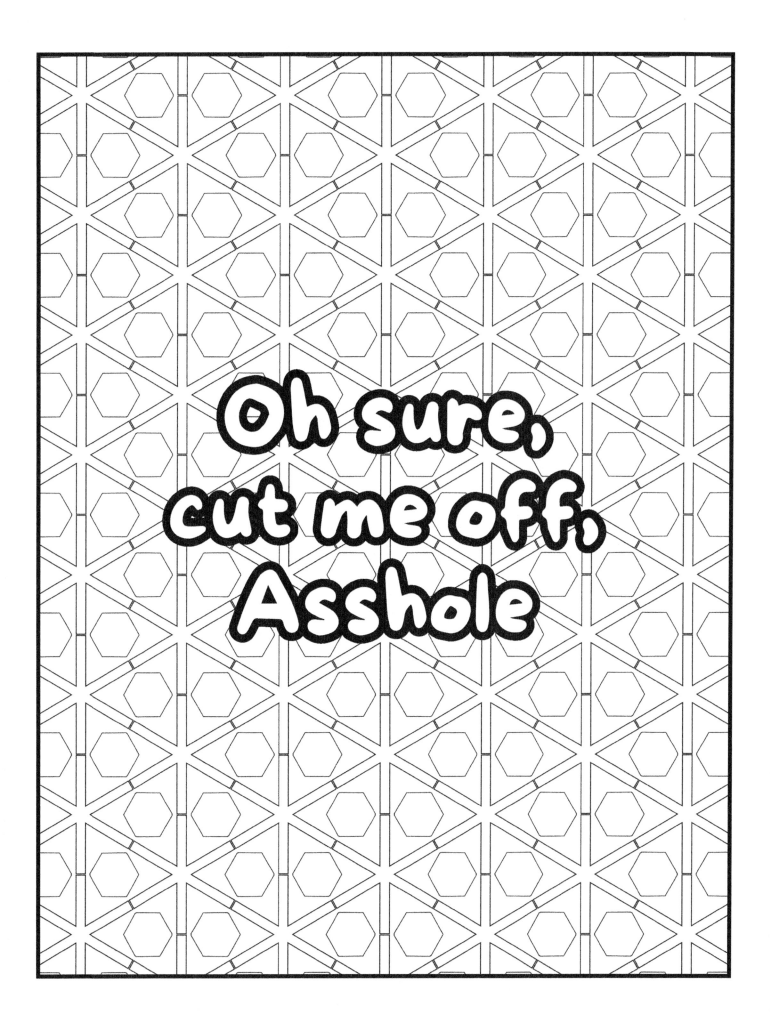

PAULEY PRESS

PAULEY PRESS

PAULEY PRESS

STOP FUCKING TEXTING AND DRIVING

PAULEY PRESS

PAULEY PRESS

Printed in Great Britain
by Amazon